Ma

Mainland

Chris Searle

CALDER & BOYARS

LONDON

First published in Great Britain 1974
by Calder & Boyars Ltd
18 Brewer Street London W1R 4AS

ISBN 0 7145 1069 6

Printed in Great Britain by
Whitstable Litho

CONTENTS

2. Home

ACKNOWLEDGEMENTS

To Norman Hidden, friend and teacher, for permission
  to include *Boys* and *Stepney Plane Trees,* first published
  in WORKSHOP.
To INK for *To Stephen McCarthy.*
To STEPNEY WORDS for *Brick Desh.*
To BRECHT TIMES for *Stepney Strength* and *Well Met*
To RACE TODAY for *Assembly*
To FROZEN ARAB'S SOCK for *Bus of Smiles*
To TRIBUNE for *No Recruiting Song*

To my Mother and Father

MAINLAND

Now I begin to peel off these false skins,
These skins that have conditioned me.
They fall away like islands,
Clippings like atolls, pared from the mainland.
Each cutting makes the crescent, tree-lined shore
Come nearer like an outstretched arm, beckoning,
Until I see beyond the reefs, the pounding surf
To something I can call myself,
Held between the arms of brothers.

I have read of islands, thought of islands.
I have lived on islands, loved on islands.
I have been an island, making myself the fount of life,
The object and subject of myself,
The island of escape, of easy isolation,
Of uncommitment to a huger mass
That always surrounded me while I did not speak.

Now I have sailed, and desperately swum,
Making strokes towards my friends,
Whose strokes made trenches through the waves between us,
And we crashed from the surf
Gasping, laughing, hugging together
And found, and were this mass,
This sand and earth of heads and flesh
This one mind with the voices of multitudes,
This mainland, us too, this mainland.

If this was a voyage, it sailed by needs,
Beginning from an island in the void
An English void, degenerate, possessed,
A void of self where self was all,
Trapped by self in dreary, self-enchanting study —
We were only selves then, eating, drinking
Knowledge that made more self of words and brain.

That time is gone, that island sunken,
Friend, I move inside you.
We stamp along the main, beside each other.

Part 1

AMERICA

THE IMMIGRANTS

In their day, after the wars,
They knew things were hard,
So they came looking for comfort
In a huge, new idea,
Which they called a land.

Or they came from eastern Europe,
Humbly and quietly,
To lose their pain
And lose the name
Of displaced persons.

Squashed in their tenement houses
Or blitzed homes,
The new space and new money
Seemed holy to them.

They did not come
As discoverers or adventurers,
To found another country
Or grow a new soul,
They came for comfort and possession,
Bringing their old life
And their old Christmases
And their old dreams of home
With them, in their suitcases.

They came for the old life
In a new way, with new securities,
And the separate house
With the rumpus room in the basement,
And the stereo and the Pontiac
And the photographic equipment
They always wanted,
In a strange land with only a name.

And now they meet in their clubs and homes
In proud, ethnic upkeep,
To find assimilation only in dollars,

And arm themselves against the generous risks
Of too much that is new,
While their children take their courses
And get their credits
And dance in discotheques.

Hamilton, Ontario. 1966

JOHNNY

I jus' sit up here and look down at the city —
See there boy, see the skyway bridge,
And the lake right past it over there,
And jeez, if you look, right over there
You can see Tronno —
Shit, not today I guess it's too hazy,
But often you get a good view of the tall buildings —
Wan' a beer? Sure, they're on me
I always keep a couple here, right under these ol' steps,
I gotta be careful though,
Don' want no guy to see me drinking.
Yeh, I'm always up here, have been for months —
Supposed to be fixin' this bit of highway here,
But I guess I only work ten or twelve minutes out of eight
                              hours.
All them fuckin' Italyans after my job —
Now one's my fuckin' foreman,
Jeez, a guy's gotta be careful —
Hey, you're not mad if I swear are you?
Sure, me too, that's great.
Yeh, it's a good place this, sure it is —
You'll like it here,
Yeh, it's a good city, they call it the Steel city, know that?
See all that down there, that's Stelco —
Steel Company of Canada, yeh
Biggest steel joint in the country.
Yeh,
I never been so happy as I am now, —
And I done all kinds of things.
Las' year I worked down there at Fort Elgin
On a fur farm, — yeh, shitty work.
And 'fore that I was in the Rockies, jeez,
Working down there on the CPR   —
Jeez, all them mountains —
I used to know all their names,

Can't remember any now.
I guess I got no money now really,
Just enough to get what I want —
Got a little room down there in Melbourne Street —
You can see the place from here,
Yeh, see it right down there, follow my finger,
Down there near that Safeway store,
See it — Yeh that's it.
I got enough for my room and enough for the beer,
I don' give a shit now —
Jeez, I have to watch that fuckin' leg,
I caught it under a cabinet yesterday.
Yeh, you got to keep movin' in this country,
No good sittin' mopin' —
I was married, sure — made the wrong choice I guess.
I brought her home all the money
And she never quitted naggin',
Yeh, got two sons too —
Don't know exactly where they are,
Out west somewhere.
Shit, they're okay, they're just fine
I got insurance on 'em —
It's all paying for their education,
And if they don' go to school,
Then it all comes back to me.
'Part from that
I guess I don' have a pot to piss into.
Okay boy, well, I guess I'll be here tomorrow,
I'm always here,
I only jus' sit up here and look down over the city.

Hamilton, Ontario. 1966

MAN POWER

Even the concept seems ridiculous —
'Unemployed in Canada',
But these men wait for jobs,
And now the myths are blasted.

By now they have got used to misconceptions —
That this land will give them all they want,
And so, they wait for jobs,
Swearing in strange accents, as they stamp around the sidewalks.

They were here yesterday, and all last week,
Never bothering to form a queue,
And yet, they wait for jobs
And turn up their collars, as the snow drizzle falls.

Thinking of their life insurance bills
They see others stepping from their Oldsmobiles,
And yet they wait for jobs
Because they have no magic papers.

Walking through revolving doors, in grey suits
Young men stride, joking with their typists,
But these men wait for jobs,
And curse a country that does not seem to care.

The lure is dead, that once persuaded them
To come to Canada and give their strengths,
And now they wait for jobs,
While old muscles droop, and coughs break up their breath.

Hamilton, Ontario. 1966

TORONTO WINTER

A strange kind of coldness here.
Perhaps it is the pervasive
Damp from the lake,
Creeping into the frosty vitals
Of the city.

Perhaps it is the clipped,
Smooth surfaces of the buildings
Straight up from the streets
With no decor or ostentation
To hold warmth.

Perhaps it is the unconcerning
Briskness of the pace of the
People's walk, or the smooth
Mobility of the cars that move so
Automatically.

Perhaps it is the greyness
Of the clothes the people wear,
And their neat compactness
That keeps in the heat
For themselves.

Toronto, Ontario. 1967

CORK TOWN

Here, by the tracks
Of the Buffalo rail,
In a green parlour,
Irishmen weep
Into their standard glasses
Of carbonated beer,
Talking of Dublin
And their old snugs
And the women at home.

On St Patrick's Day
They serve green beer,
And old songs come
With every demonstration of remembrance,
With the snow sinking into the earth outside
And the train shunting through
The rotting, wooden homes they bought.
Here are the immigrants,
Twenty, thirty years after,
Still drinking into
The cliches of nostalgia.

Hamilton, Ontario. 1967

C.N.R.

Ten hours past Toronto,
It seems a dark world is being blown to me,
Primeval forests loom outside
As I drink up with some soldiers,
And at a place called Capreol
I flake out until we reach Winnipeg,
And there we buy a crate of beer.

Good and pissed across the prairies
As the yellow flatness turns to gold —
When you are young and drunk and crashing through
The new space of the world,
With nothing fixed in your life,
And people are showing you themselves
As if they know that this will be your only meeting,
And you must know all.

And they wish you good luck in this great mass of earth,
And a fat, beaming woman gives you a lucky dollar,
And an old railwayman winks and passes you a cigar,
And a young, pale nun says she will pray for you
That you will soon find work —
And I believe her as I see this generosity,
This mainland all around me.

And talking to the trainman,
Who came from near me in England, a Londoner
Now turned priest of Canada as it whirls past —
And he takes me to the cab and sits me with the driver,
And the fireman shares his coffee
And sweet, ripe peaches from the Okanagan.

I see the sun rising in West Saskatchewan,
And the swamp birds on the line before the engine
Scattering as the train rumbles towards them,
And flapping back to their low lakes.

And I seem to be dividing the world,
Cutting through unfallen hugenesses
Like one of the Earth's inheritors
There, with twenty dollars in my pocket,
As mountains pass, beckoning me with invitations,
And I take in the wild scent of the pines.

In a line drawn across a continent
The great train tears onwards, looking for the sea,
Following a grey, loping river through grim canyons
As it plunges through the mainland,
Carrying me with the mainland.

Canada, 1967

EDMONTON

It seemed like a boom city,
So I stopped there, and tried to find a job.

A lady in Real Estate told me
Yes, a smart young man
Can make his fortune here —
And she showed me her house
In the suburbs of town, next to the river —
Don't you think it's cute? she said,
And look at the garden, do you like my barbecue?
I guess that corner
There, by the fishpond
Is the best place for it.

An eskimo, who had made it good
In Public Relations,
Said to me, stick around man,
Yeh, any guy can make it here,
Look at me.
And he smiled from his high cheekbones
Dusted down his suit
And bought me a cocktail.

The mayor told me from the radio,
Grinning through his intonation,
Yes, the city had shown a completely new
Skyline
In the last ten years,
And was on the wave of greatness.

Three testaments, spoken in gladness
Under the dollar's favourite shrine.

1967

SPIT

It is a worrying thing,
To have a little boy
Not much older than a baby
Approach you on a crowded bus,
Leer at you,
And spit out straight in your face
'Hippie',
As if that word meant Satan or Death
Or the bogey man,
While the grinning parents
At the front of the bus,
With white, clean faces,
Call him back proudly.

Or to walk across a bridge in the snow
As a truck passes,
And to see a wholesome face in the cab
Spit at you with eyes of hate,
And feel a globule of phlegm
Resting on your collar.

                    Calgary, Alberta, 1968

FOOTMAN

Yes boy, I'll have a drink with you —
Just one mind, I only came in for half an hour,
I don't really like these places,
Look at those blokes, they just get drunk
And slither around and fight and shout,
But at least you can still find a quiet corner like this,
Can't you?
Yes, I'm going back to Vancouver tomorrow,
I only came here to see my young brother —
He had a stroke last week, you know,
He's in the veterans' hospital here,
Yes, he's always lived here,
Ever since the war —
Too cold for me here, too much snow,
I like the coast —
But I think he's going now.
Yes, I had another brother . . .
We joined up together, all three —
You know, we'd come out here together
About five years before then —
Jack, Tom and me.
Yes, we all enlisted — in the Kootenays.
Jack and me — Jack's in the hospital —
We went in the infantry, but Tom was different,
You see, he always liked machines
So he went with the tanks.
Yes, Tom went with the tanks,
And they were new and unreliable then, you know,
Were always blowing up.
So before he went, old Tom said to me —
I was single then you know — he said
That if anything happened to him with those tanks
Would I marry his wife and look after his boy.
And that's what happened, you see —

Tom went with the tanks to Cambrai,
And they got him there,
And she's been a good wife to me
All these years.
Yes, nineteen-o-seven it was
When I came out here —
Yes, I was twenty-three.
Back home I was a footman,
Yes, to the Earl of Romney down in Sussex —
Yes, he was a kind man, always kind,
But no, that was no life, was it?
So I came out here.
C.P.R, yes, after a time I worked for them —
Forty years a trainman —
And even now they look after me.
They give me a pension,
And I've got a little house in Vancouver.
Oh, yes, free travel —
It didn't cost me a cent to come here.
Look at this card,
I can travel all over the country with this —
Yes, C.P, C.N — Great Northern too,
And some of the American lines,
I can go all around.
And sometimes that's what I do,
Just ride round for a week
To see how things have changed.
The best line, well,
You should see that stretch of rail
To Prince Rupert, that's where I first worked.
Yes, B.C. was wild then, and beautiful —
For my first three years there, I never worked —
I never had to.
See, I built a shack outside of Vancouver,
There were no suburbs then, no big buildings —
It was only a small place,
So different now, so different.
See, I never hardly had to work —

I mean, not what you'd call work,
It was all there for me.
Good Lord, I got up early
And dug clams or went fishing —
I could pick blueberries and wild strawberries,
I could hunt and shoot what I wanted,
I had my own garden —
Why should I work?
Of course, you can't do that now,
That's all gone now,
But you know how I felt then, well
I knew I wasn't a footman any more.

                    Calgary, Alberta. 1968

CALGARY

Build towers from your oil
To glorify your pride
In the fabric of the flimsy greatness
Which you blast about yourself
On your radios,
Which are the organs of your ego.

The stampede of conceit
Which you, among the foothills,
Call civic pride,
Stamps against your growth
As you force,
Without the roots of humility
An uncreated shape
From your panoply of civilisation.

You have to clink your dollars loud
To make the mountains hear you
And notice you are there.
Look at them, they say nothing,
Yet are massively there,
And have a solidness for their frequency
Which laughs at you.

1968

MAN AND CAT

In a quivering midnight,
A shout from the darkness
Of a murky street,
And slurring sounds that missed
The breaks and pauses to separate words,
And a shape reels towards me.

A man in a hairy jacket
And checked collar,
His eyes bright, his face obscure,
His teeth intermittent,
Thrusts a cat at me.
'Take the cat', he said.

A cat in my hands,
The slits of its eyes shining
Like vertical rods of light,
And the man saying,
'Take it, take it,
He's been mine for two years
But tomorrow I leave,
So you must take it'.

A truck lurches past
Filling the night with roars
As the cat purrs in my hands.
I stammer and slur
As if I am drunk and fighting for words,
'I can't do that,
I'm leaving myself'.

The long grunt of desperation,
The loud sprawling words of anger:
'They all say that, they all move on.
No-one stops, they're all moving.

No-one has time. No-one stops
For even a cat'.

Standing in a road, I am accused.
Open-mouthed, I only mutter,
' . . find someone who lives here'.
'They all say that.
They all move on.
No-one, no-one wants to know'.

And he grabbed the cat,
And his eyes poured tears
And the cat mewed,
As he shuffled back
Into the darkness.

Whitehorse, Yukon. 1968

INDIANS IN A BEER PARLOUR

And the man at the bar
Does not smile
As he keeps the tap running.

And the man with the tray
Does not talk
As he keeps the beer coming,

To drunken men
Who only put out their hands
With crumpled dollars,
With their thirst drumming
On their senses
And breaking the skin
As it drenches the soul.

On paleface beer
They lean and leer
Through open mouths
And lolling tongues
Slobber beneath
Hair and grease.
Thick hands paw willing women
And mouths gnaw on peanuts —
The victuals of enclosure,
To keep fat
In the squeezing, unloved compound
Of their keepers.

Men of dignity, sons of the warrior
They poison you slowly, they undermine your beauty,
They make you drink the waters of perishment.
America! When will you thrive without genocide?

Whitehorse, Yukon. 1968

PROSPECTORS

Four young Yugoslavs,
New Canadians with their English grammar books,
Searching for work in the unopened mines,
Stammering out their half-sentences
With great hopes in the Great North,
They came to its city of great prices,
Prefabricated in the bellowing hugeness
With its monuments to past gold.

Four weeks waiting, their savings ebbing,
They wait for the mines to open,
And pay eight dollars each
Every day
For a quarter of a small room
To a grey-haired man with spectacles,
Like five hundred others, protracting their chances
In this city of waiting brawn.

And as they put out their thumbs for three thousand miles,
Leaving thoughts of sealed mines,
Searching for the South
Like others before them
With empty pockets,
Breathing mispronounced curses along a gravel highway,
They only move along a well-trod route
Of disappointment.

Whitehorse, Yukon. 1968

KLONDIKE

Ice on the Yukon River
About to crack and move,
Takes in the setting sun
To itself.

Tumbling saloons list
Into streets of mud,
And puddles show the long shadow
Of the slant.

All the girls, all the pans
Gone with the people
Who left before the
Death.

Wood mutilating itself,
Waiting for the fire,
Sluggish wrecks
Slow to die.

Broken shacks
Sprawl in dying attitudes
Along the river
By abandoned hulks,

And Indians move
Within the debris
And their children play
With plastic toys.

Days of gold, gone.
Beneath the darkening hills
Only a death-rotting
Glory.

Dawson City, Yukon. 1968

HASHBURY

In Golden Gate's panhandle
They squat cross-legged
Or sprawl on balding lawns
And smile beatifically as you pass,
Reversing the prevailing aggression.
So you sit with them, and they cool you down
With their attitudes of giving.
Oranges and chocolate are passed to you,
And for a few suspended moments
You feel you are with Jesus or
Sitting at the feet of the sage
You have been chasing all your life.
They offer you a smoke, while all around
The traffic rattles, and you marvel at
Their lack of caution as police stare
From cars that gleam on all sides,
And you feel like glorifying them
For their nonchalence.
I just came out, anyway, one says,
And if they put me back again
Then I guess I'll have a cool time
Cuz all my buddies are there —
The jails are full man,
They can't stop us,
You see man, we're slowly winning.
Psst, do you have some speed?
Speed is king here —
Kittens from a sack are swapped
For an ounce
By a boy and girl just up from San Diego
For a summer at the scene.
Someone warns them,
Go easy with that stuff brother,
It's strong man, and I guess
She's only a young chick so

Stay with her, while she blows.
They seem to have their concepts of
Protection.
Man, my chromosomes are in
Good shape, don't get hung up for me.
And they almost convinced,
In their supreme unconcern,
As if they had a world of sustenance
Behind them, or a strong guard of God.
Hair and robes:
Strange harbingers,
In their stance of seers,
Sitting in their groups like portents
Of some waylaid divinity,
Giving invitations to
The holiness of dissipation.

                    San Francisco, 1968.

JANIS JOPLIN AND THE HOLDING COMPANY AT A HELL'S ANGELS' DANCE, CAROUSEL BALLROOM, SAN FRANCISCO

Outside, the eyes of police
Eat through visors
Ready for riots
And manoeuvres of hatred.

Angels, great bears of oil
With maltese crosses,
Floundering marshals
Of their own revels,

With their badges glowing
In the strobe lights, advance —
Blasting somewhere
All your order.

Fat, greasy trunks
Made flaccid with a sedentary saddle life,
Grapple between each other's leather
And grind on the floor

To music which tears the mind
And crushes control,
Thrashing its sounds across your head
Until you surrender.

Mouths drool, slobber for chaos
Puked across the floor,
Until you beg your senses
To stop themselves.

A hall of loping, crawling movements
Reeling and breaking away,
Crashing through doors and windows
In frantic gropes to leave the mass.

Fragments breaking off
All with the sickness of decay,
Pumping out the pus
Of a metaphor of America.

1968

SOLDIERS

I see them on the buses,
I see them on the trains,
The planes, the roads, the restaurants —
Soldiers.

Young men, perplexed.
Staring at their own uniforms in bewilderment,
Wondering how they were ever
Soldiers.

Now exposed, the skin on the backs of their necks
Shivers, as they gaze
At the plaques on their breasts, which tell them
Their names.

Some, quiet and self-conscious,
Read philosophy through their glasses,
Taking themselves away from the threatening world
Of action.

Talk to them,
They do not try to vindicate themselves,
They only hope their term will be
In Germany or Spain.

Vietnam: the name rings in their ears
Like Death knocking at their suburb,
Making it a place of sudden, violent
Life.

They are not humorous about their chances,
One in ten will go there, they say,
And some of those will
Die.

There is something in their eyes,
Which is not doubt,
Because they have no doubts, they are
Unwilling.

Their looks are mirrors of defeat,
They move laggingly, like prisoners.
They do not look like
Soldiers.

America, 1968

TED

You tell me about being there
And standing in the chopper's door
Horribly vulnerable,
And firing in fits of madness
To save yourself and your friends.

You show me the scars
And the holes in your stomach
Stretching round to your back,
And you say you were six months
In a hospital bed.

You tell me of the bodies of your buddies,
Their mouths filled with their own balls,
That you found significantly placed
On jungle trails.

You say it has made you sick
To fill the throats of strange young men with water,
And hold them while they struggle and choke
And spew out what you need to know.

You say that in those callous swamps
You have learned to recognise Evil,
And you saw it clear, tangible, obvious,
In those Cong.

And you say you have been exhausted with compassion,
That out there your pity has multiplied
For those people you have helped,
And you would go back there again.

And you talk about how she loves you,
Your girl in Saigon,
And you say that the legend is true,

That they are, doubtlessly,
The most beautiful girls in the world.

Ted, where is your analysis?
It is only your senses that speak.
But I also have been an onlooker,
I have known the cameras of the world
And oppressed words from those you bombed.
I do not discount them Ted,
They are my signals.

Seattle, Washington. 1968

TEOTIHUACAN

Up, up monuments of holiness
To find the sun with stone
And scale rocks to the moon.
Pyramids. Shapes of wild devotion,
Their roots in the plains,
Trunks sweeping high to Heaven,
Organic blocks of man and God
Fused.

Dead avenues of broken lava,
Widths of gone volcanic glory
Sprawled inert beneath flat hills
And plateaux of stern priests,
Who stare from their centuries
On us, who climb their stone,
Carrying our guide books to their
Massiveness.

Stone butterflies held to the Earth
By their weight of sacred love
To grinning snakes with plumes
To change them into Air,
Invaded by new devotees,
To whom each stone of worship is a curio
Cut from a frenzied love of deprived
Antiquity.

Now, with a new flamboyance, she steps.
Some new goddess from
The new border in the North,
Spraying the steps to the Sun
With strange rites of words and colours
Worrying to those sacred blocks,
Making old, forged, shapen sanctities
Uncreate.

Teotihuacan, Mexico. 1968

ROBERT KENNEDY

With my two German friends in Veracruz,
Walking round the city,
Telling people we are not Americanos
When they tell us that we are.
'No, Aleman y Inglese', we say,
And they stop, amazed —
'Aleman y Inglese?' they say,
'No es posible',
Why don't we kick and shoot
And kill each other, and
What is happening in the war,
And is Hitler still winning?
And as we talk and drink and laugh together,
And drift from bar to bar,
Their amazement seems irrelevant.

But as we sit in the plaza
And watch pretty Mexican girls with black eyes
Parade arm in arm
And give coy smiles behind strict manners,
And listen to the blend of voices and marimbas
As sailors stagger drunkenly to the whorehouses,
Somebody behind us says
Kennedy es muerto
Kennedy es muerto,
And suddenly the words are screened above us,
Words of yellow flickering light on a black bank,
As people scream and rush to its radiance
Of neon news that cripples a continent —
And the flow stops and
The whole of life is suspended,
As we curse in our mutual perplexity
And writhe at the enormities of America,
Mourning through the ugly compact of the Church.

And a brother's soldiers still kill on
By Mekong's waters, deaths untolled:
Men whose only bank was comradeship.

Veracruz, Mexico. 1968

COCKROACHES

Outside, the river slimes by
And in my mind
Alligators crawl up the banks
And gnaw the hotel walls.

Today, I saw a man in the plaza,
A trick cyclist
Who danced like a god cavorting,
Leaps from a moving saddle
Praising his life of balance,
Stunning pirouettes
With an ecstacy of fineness,
While people clapped.

Sweat all over me
As I wriggle on dirty sheets
And curse the tropics.
Jerk the frayed string —
And there is light,
And twenty cockroaches
Running on my chest.

Villahermosa, Mexico. 1968

NEW ORLEANS

Now, synthetic swings
And psychedelic fantasies
Brood along Bourbon Street,
And crass sounds
Of go-go music, and flabby bellies
Working folds each side of their navels,
Tempt the people looking for a good time
Amongst the iron lace.
The old world is gone,
Except for one or two dusty places
Where gnarled fingers still love their instruments
And the music they play,
And creole faces show their own transcension
Of the music they create,
Where they sit in modesty
Directing the soberness of perfect sounds
Arranged for their seven pieces.
And as Saturday night crashes
With the anxious heartiness
Of forced, unreal happiness in the street outside,
And the desperation within the soul
Leaks out in the attitudes of aggression
Emerging with the waving cans and bottles
And frothing mouths —
Inside a rough, unnoticed room
Bugle Call and Dippermouth
Savoy and Muskrat Ramble
And Just a Closer Walk with Thee
Ring out like the revolt of order
In a cracking, grasping land.

1968

JACKSON SQUARE

Sitting by myself,
Having a smoke in Jackson Square,
Watching a small bird
On the mane of Jackson's horse
As he doffs his hat —
And suddenly beside me
A beautiful girl
With long black hair
Holding an iced lollipop
Out to me.
'Take it please', she said,
'I always do this
When I see people
Who seem to be lonely'.

Sitting by myself
Having a smoke on the levee
Watching the boats spread their wash below me —
I saw a man, with cropped hair
And a black skin,
Looking hunched and angry
And spitting in the water.
'What's up, mate?' I said,
And he scowled, 'I've no job here,
Fucking whitey
Won't give me one'.

Here, in America,
On this mainland,
There are many shapes of people.

New Orleans, 1968

GREYHOUND

Beside me, a young Jewish boy
Hung up about his
Puerto Rican girlfriend
Pours out worried confessions.
In front, a white soldier
Tells me about the Cong
Sitting in the trees right above him
Who nearly ripped open his crutch
With their bullets.
Behind me, a black soldier
Smoothes away
With a brown-skinned girl
He has just met
Who smiles as he says, Shit man,
I'm not going out there.
And near Winston-Salem
We blow a tyre
And we all get out
And push together.

North Carolina. 1968

RESPECT

America
Takes its memorials very seriously.
Washington
A city of sepulchres and ghettoes,
Arlington
A national park of dead men.
Jack's grave
A mecca for Americans
Bringing homage to their saint.
Family happy-snaps
Against the backcloth of Jack's words
Written in stone, over his tomb.
And now above his bones
They shout and laugh and prance
And chew gum, and eat cookies —
While Bobby, three weeks dead,
Rots quietly, down the slope,
Ten yards away.

1968

RAP ON

Outside the fences
By stagnant, ornamental water,
A white man from the University
Lectures on Gandhi,
And tells his listeners
That the King liked him.

He talks straight
Of methods that won,
And gives information
Of strategies of peace,
To fight for rights, he says,
Without bullets.

Black men rise
And shake their arms,
And one interrupts
And holds the meeting —
And rap on brother,
It's your turn now.

'And my black brothers
You listen to me —
What's this Gandhi, man?
Where's this at, man?
We aint heard
Of no Gandhi'.

'Yeah, rap on brother,
Rap on more,
'Cuz these white brothers
Is gonna feel us soon,
And it won't be no Gandhi
When we come'.

Outside the fences
The white man tries again —
But he can't go on.
So he puts on his jacket
And walks away quietly
Clutching his notes.

Washington, 1968

BEDFORD-STUYVESANT

Subterranean shops with wooden boards
Hide their windows,
Black men in broken doorways
Cast lethargic attitudes,
Cinemas with burnt-out lobbies
Show no posters,
Men with large black dogs
Slide along the sidewalks.

In the back seat of a white Cadillac
Floating up the Styx to Brooklyn Broadway,
Under black girders and spars which rumble,
Showing no sky or no green or no sun,
Only black above and all around,
And Aretha shouting for freedom.

Charred bodies of wrecked cars
Sprawl dead in the gutters,
Street signs bent back double
Give opposite directions,
Girls with slogans on their sweaters
Move precociously,
Mutilated blocks with smashed windows
Gawk in agony.

In the back seat of a white Cadillac,
Crouching in a capsule of hate,
Feeling the beer cans rattle on the chasse,
Reading the lips of swearing people
While sounds fill up the car with dented fury,
Telling me to reach out in this darkness.

Tight pants with back pockets
Conceal well-shaped buttocks
Dark eyes are not exposed
Behind large shades,

Bright turtle-necks and swinging medallions
Shine off the windscreen,
Black faces crowd the intersections
With armed scowls.

In the back seat of a white Cadillac,
Inside a cockpit heated with arrogance,
Sealed by our own grimaces from the hate outside
As synthetic sounds clang out with mindless fury
And mousy female voices squeaking in a studio,
With plastic anthems socking summer to me.

Brooklyn, 1968

EARLY MORNING

I wake with the city's arms around me.
Outside the window, garbage cans clang
With a kind of displaced harmony.
Looking down, direct, through black steel zeds
Of fire escapes like someone's scaffold —
Kids in tee-shirts play in the chasm,
And shout on the sidewalks of an empty block.
Even here, if you catch the moments,
There are lulls of peace before the day takes arms.

New York, 1968

NEW YORK

Queue at the Greyhound station,
Waiting for the Boston bus.
Underground fumes stimulate uneasy tempers
Already riled by the late bus.
The queue grows longer,
Filling with a fast belligerence·
As people note noisily
The capacity is passed.
Bus pulls up casually, an hour late.
Driver steps down in impeccable uniform,
Grey cap with shiny peak, large shades —
Confronts passengers with offhand apologies
Met with shouts of petulance.
A rush for the gate —
An American stampede, like those I read about.
Cases and metal trunks crash against
Brittle bones of an old lady
And soil the white smock
Of a frightened nun.
Feet stamp and tread down a little girl
Disconnected from her mother, crying in pain
As hard thighs and knees smash her face
And stun her faith
Leaving only perplexity.
Drivers block the gate, pressing angrily
Bastard, Sonofabitch, Motherfucker,
Flailing out in indignation, dignities assaulted.
A mass of seething pettinesses
Breaking to hysteria
An America of swearing women
Losing their warmth, unmothering themselves
With snapping, spitting dogs of men —
Eyes blowing hate across a bus station,
And thrashing arms, heaving violence,
The many stilted sides of aggression.

1968

SKID ROW

Outside huge towers of light,
Exhausted pits, eyes of darkness stare
And crawl like black crabs over worn faces —
While sprightly people step past,
Wearing badges for their favourites.

Propped by dingy porches,
In their own sanctuaries
They hold fast to grimy bottles,
And esoteric judgements pass from face to face
As the world steps by with its slogans.

'Yeah, when I get me outa here,
I got cousins in Canada —
They got a farm in B.C.
An' I guess I'm headin' there
In a month or two'.

White liquid tilts inside the bottles
And runs fast down stretched throats,
As stomachs heave inwards to themselves,
And collapsing, cover leather belts
When the bare arm falls away.

Unswept sidewalks —
Beds for fallen people,
While men choose presidents
And go for rings
Around the moon.

Chicago, 1968

MIAMI BEACH

Women under untold thicknesses
Of suffocating powder
And barrels of heaving scent,
Chins like beaks
And sunglasses like monsters' eyes —
Staving off Age's serenity
And inevitability,
Croak along,
Exhibited in parades of ghastliness,
Chaperoned by ball-paunched husbands
With money.

America, this is your endland,
Here you finish.

1968

FLYING OVER CUBA

Down there is Fidel
And the tracks of Che.
And look! The coastline
Of a map I once knew.

Why do I miss out this island?
Why is Caribair not Cuban air?
Why do the flights and fares
Connecting these islands
Exclude that blurring surf below?

What I will see next
Will not be Cuba,
Jamaica is minutes away,
The Dungle, West Kingston.

The world changes in minutes.

1968

URCHIN

Cruising around Kingston town,
With my camera tucked under my arm —
Looking for the shapes of poverty.
And there was one, right there.
A little boy with bleeding feet
Asks me for money, because I am white.
He had no shoes, and his cuts gaped
Like toothless, bloody mouths.
So we found the Bata and I bought him a pair,
As light-skinned people watched, eyeing me strangely
As they did their buying.
He came with me to the ship
And the nurse bandaged his feet,
Before I took him back to where I found him.
Then, point blank, I took out my camera
And shot him as he stared at me.

A dark woman stopped
As she passed with her shopping bag,
And with bitter stories in her eyes, she said,
'If you photograph that child
Make sure you give him something'.

I have moved since then, and in many places
I thought about my human interest
When I only documented his pathos
With chromatic blows of cheapened art —
And every time I look at the photograph,
A black, ragged, frightened boy,
Its form overcomes, and its texture
And its colour and its composition,
And I forget his agony, and his cuts seeping blood,
And his tired eyes, and his limp of underdevelopment,
And how I turned away and left him standing

On a corner, between two banks,
Staring at me, bewildered by me
Between the throbbing flow of other people.

Cruising around Kingston town,
With my camera, shot out, under my arm —
Ashamed of my liberalism and afraid to show
The first responsibility of commitment.

Kingston, Jamaica. 1968

SALLY

Sally, Peace Corps girl,
With your degree in Psychology
In a little village in the Blue Mountains,
Earnestly teaching country people
How to make baskets and co-operatives —
The code of your Americanness dictates,
And hopes to carve self-reliance all over you.
So you live alone, in a small room,
Above the village post office,
Where the insects crawl on you as you sleep,
And the people come and see you
And they ask you for your help,
And they take you for a goddess with your blonde hair,
And just like them, you must have no money,
And no record-player, and no transport.
And you live only with the people, simply,
Like your supervisor tells you, for two years.

And now as you talk, after your tour of duty,
And say how the people don't seem to like baskets,
It seems as if you are blown away from the mainland,
Wrapped in your own island.

Jamaica. 1968

ON THE CAPSIZING OF A BOAT
OFF UNION ISLAND IN THE GRENADINES

You build your hotels
With the blood of these people,
You use their hands
You use their strength
You take their islands,

America
Today your money killed
Sixty men.

You gave them wages
That you would not even give to
Your most powerless American
And an unsafe boat
To come from their island
To one you have bought
As a garden for your flabby rich.

They built your hotel
With its palm-shaded terraces
And its tiled showers
And its painted bar
With its view of the blue sea
And then you sent them home.

You found them an old boat,
It would do for them
You did not check,
You had no interest
You saved on its leaks
And on its crampedness.

When it capsized
And sixty black men drowned
You were well covered
They were not your sons
They were not your people.

America
Your heart is green
It is stiff paper
It is very crinkled
Your heart is your dollar.

America
Leave these people
Or when they are one
They will roll down their blackness upon you,
They will burst you.

                    St Vincent, 1968.

GRENADA CHRISTMAS

'Do you like these legs?' she said,
'This one is the best, it is stainless,
And never rusts, and the joints are never stiff
Even though you never oil them.
It's the most comfortable one I've ever had —
My daughter gave it me for Christmas'.
And she showed me her spare false legs,
And smiled through kind, withered skin,
As she limped out with drinks on a plastic tray,
With the frogs croaking in the road outside.

'Come to the Christmas dance with us tonight —
It's supposed to be formal, but nobody will mind you,
Because you are a stranger,
And anyway, my husband is a policeman.
Here, you can borrow a white shirt and bow tie,
It's always a good fete'.
But at the door, the man said no —
It wasn't his fault, but the dance was strictly formal,
And you haven't even got a jacket —
Couldn't you find a proper one somewhere?

Sprawling sounds filter through the window
Among the mosquitoes, as I try to sleep,
Hearing a man from Carriacou
In the next room, above the partition,
Talking to himself in political oratory,
Declaiming speeches to a heated night
Giving sounds of men beating pan
And blowing trumpets,
Jigging up the street towards my window,
Tottering with the rum inside them,
And clapping hands for Christmas.

St George's, Grenada. 1968.

BOYS

While kites eclipse the sun
And fly with the wind,
And boys haul on strings,
Keeping their toes entrenched in the sand,
Men, under roofs of palm branches,
Peruse the sea.

Boys splash in the surf
Crashing their fists against the waves —
Black fishes falling under thrashing gates of water
And coming up shaking,
While men pass nets across their knees
And look for holes.

Boys kick a ball on a hard, damp beach
And shout with screams of joy,
Pass me the ball nah man,
Pass me the ball —
While men carry cane on their shoulders
And their cutlasses shine.

Boys on bamboo rafts beyond the surf
Row along the bay,
And their friends turn somersaults through the foam
And swim towards them,
While men in gardens on the cliffside
Dig for yams.

Boys throw wood to the tops of trees,
And with long sticks, poke towards the heart
While green nuts fall like dead men,
And roll, and stop in silence —
While men whistle tunes and walk home
From the gardens.

Tobago. 1969

JUNIOR

Junior, up from the country,
Working as a servant for Mr Gomes,
Leaning on a twig broom, watching the saga boys
Bouncing with their shades along the beaches,
Liming on the corners of their dreams,
Smoking their power behind rum shop fences —
This is a new world to you.

Junior, with no certificates,
Very black, and no bright shirts,
Watching the cars go past
And the men drink up on a Friday evening —
Escape is your watchword,
Anything to escape, you say,
To get out of here, to leave this island.

Junior, when you brought me those recruitment forms,
You said this was the only way,
The US Army will get you out, you said,
Would I help you fill them in?
Did you hate me when I tore them up?
You walked out the door.
You never came back.

Tobago, 1969.

RUM SHOP

The man in the cage,
Who sits at the till
Behind his wire defences,
Giving out change through a small hole,
Watches his customers
On the wooden stalls and benches
He bought for them.

There they drink rum
And hammer their fists
On the dull surfaces
Of unsteady tables
Which rock on the floor,
As men play their Soul
On juke boxes.

And every walk across the floor
Becomes a dance,
As men stand up
And glasses crash
And voices clash
To void the sound of waves
Outside the door.

And inside small, partitioned rooms,
Clearly numbered
On hardboard walls,
Handfuls of ice rattle
From an enamel dish,
And base the draughts
Of the world of men.

Tobago, 1969

PORT OF SPAIN

Streets of hustlers and hucksters selling their city
And their watches and coconut pastries —
The world a market of trivia and trinkets
To find bread and life,
Changing hands for coins
In the sweat of a Trinidad sun.

Have you seen the girls of Trinidad?
The world's pallette:
Spectral shows of shades and colours
Clipping from their banks and offices
They swarm down Frederick Street
While you stand pinned by their beauty
Against the rails, gawking.

Beggars, all dark, scrawny hands towards you.
Bent, night agony in a shop doorway
As you walk home, cruising with your rum inside you.
Defeated shapes of people,
Dying in their life of suppliance.

Have you been to the fetes in Trinidad?
Have you seen them drink and dance?
Whirling to each other's gyres
And frenzied shakes of mad pulsations.
Soul, man,
Or an escape from it, to the body's heat.

Galvanise skies step from East Dry River,
Hills of piled smells and greenswill gutters
And mangy skins of dogs who wander
Like prophets of their dry country.
And snarl for their sustenance.

Have you heard the sounds of Trinidad?
Dried grass in Woodford Square
Knows shouts of black-skinned oratory,
Cursing bland faces of sno-cone eaters and carnivallers
Who never dared to reverse the centuries' hatreds
And bite back.

Broad cars thicken streets
Thick with crushed people,
And shop windows with pedestalled appliances,
Pray to oil and the tourist without blushes —
America has many disciples,
And she is one of them.

Have you seen the skins of Trinidad?
An equal place for every creed and race sounds good,
With the sun to fuse all
Into one island mesh of throbbing humanity,
While black frowns split the rays of this
Uneasy harmony.

1969

FREDERICK STREET

Up Frederick Street, we walk together
I am a white man, at least that's what they call me.
But the children know better —
'White?' they say, 'White? You're not white,
With a nose like that,
Hibiscus red, from taking the sun,
You're no white man'.
And she is black, doubtlessly black,
And her skin shines like the moon striking night
As it leaves the darkness behind the headland,
And beats its radiance
Over the undulant, breaking sea.

So we walk along together,
And on this street where young men lean,
Prurience wags like it was pleased,
And snorts are blown through sedentary noses
Of limers leaning in doorways,
And a voice in the back stabs its hate,
'Boy, you have a nice black girl there.
Wh'appen boy? Where you taking she boy?
Up by she, boy? Somewhere nice, boy?'
I wonder if he thought,
Ah, after all these years,
At last, at last,
Now we hold the whip, and we will crack it.

Port of Spain, Trinidad. 1969

BEACH FIRE (For Pete and Ros)

Last night, we built a fire on a beach.
Seizing palm fronds and logs and dried
Husks of coconuts, it blazed out of the reach
Of the sweeping, moonlit, cracking tide.
As it drooped, and burned low, we scoured
The fringe of the beach for more fuel,
And threw on flotsam, which roared
Like voices swept from mystery, real
And strong beneath the richest moon.
There it lived, and it had the seal
Of permanence, bright and fierce, and soon
The flames danced like waking dreams
And flew to smoke across our eyes.
And we relaxed, and absorbed the beams
Of loving warmth, which grew to be our prize.

But creeping forward, soaking all the dust,
The tide turned, staring at the moon,
The only mistress of the blind lust
It showed to our fire, swamping the sticks
In gradual, cruel gestures of tyrannic
Laughing, with the rhythmic crack of surf
Smothering the new, glowing birth of redness.
We piled and piled and ran in madness
To find more fuel to feed the glimpse of life
We had created from a moment's whim,
With frantic gestures, only causing strife
Amongst ourselves, as we shouted and blamed
The death on her, or me, or him,
Or the force from the sea, dark and unnamed
That sent the crawling tide over damp, charred wood
That used to hold our flames.

Rockly Bay, Tobago. 1969

PELICANS

In the careful, folding glare
Of the drooping sun, they dive,
Straight shafts of steeled light
Impaling the sea with their arrowheads,
Harpoons into the soft belly of the waves;
And today I watch the pelicans.
I see their wings flapping like great grey sail
In their long glides of easy audacity,
Pressing inside the spaces of the waves
Yet touching no water.

Men, they are blind to your island,
They only watch the sea
And the moving shape, the quick glint beneath,
With downward eyes half along their beaks
Looking through their jaws.

They have no eyes for this deformity
As the trees are mauled to death, their roots ripped
By foreign, gruesome tractors.
And the beach becomes a lost battlefield
With all the earthworks of a venal strategy
Of patterned trenches and flagged, square ditches
To base the inns and throne rooms of exploitation
For the courts and straw-crowned, bleached empresses,
And white, greasy kings with untold cameras
Of your own sold land.

They come in state with their flight bags
And horn-rimmed eyes, bedecked
In their Bermuda robes,
Seekers of a brown-skinned week
To show their friends at home
Round coke and slides and nuts and popcorn
In a corner-lighted, wooded rumpus room.

With a small corner of your sight, pelicans,
You see them to the one side
That always flies along the beach.
You do not consider them as you fall
Like rebel angels, with only the waves to break you
As the sun burns the sea.

You have seen an age of slaves, pelicans,
And have grappled with the gulls
For your own spiked fish,
While men talked easily of freedom,
But only saw their island stay the same
With white-skinned, hard-skinned men
Who beam in their unctuous avarice,
And nod to their new black slaves
To carry the bags for the gentleman
And serve him from a polished tray
And show him the whiteness of their polished teeth.

And you have dived on, pelicans,
Keeping your side of the beach,
While new, strange monuments have risen above
The carefully preserved, authentic island palms
To keep the island atmosphere
For cocktails and a well-rehearsed romance,
Available on easy terms
From the agent in the downtown shopping mall.

But your element is not inviolate, pelicans.
Where you dive and flash and fall
And keep your unawareness sacred,
There are new fish, and glassy undersides
And plastic men with tubes that strike your wings,
As you glide into them.

So today I watch the pelicans,
And speculate upon their sensitivity,
As a vanishing beauty moves to one side,
And the waves rise thick, to unknown rhythms
On the other.

Great Courland Bay, Tobago. 1969

CARNIVAL

Last night, in the clotted air
Of tropical nights, I heard the pans ringing.
Somewhere in the darkness, from a tent they sounded,
Inside the frogs and buzzing insects —
Chimes of mellow warmth and softness.

So different now,
Away from nights that close up the world
With their walls of close, thick sweat
And crawling, scuttling things,
To the blazing day and far horizons.

For now they pound in the terrible sun
For it is Carnival,
And only the day's endless equanimity
Can take that sound of crashing life,
Tearing men who move from those who watch.

Anticipation leads life through sober moments,
And days of harness, hours of dullness
Long majorities of unexcitement
Now broken in these throbbing seconds
And man beats out his will and takes his urge, his life.

Inside the sound of clang, inside that wheel
Struck by rhythmic, naked, iron want —
What desperation, what unleashings here
From daily quietness, from daily habits
Dangling through the days of life?

Lips which suck the horn of rum
Bawl out their phrases, while the waves lap
All along their path, and back again
To where they started —
Painted indians running to the fire.

All through the day they run, they dance,
And patterns press their notes against the sun
With stunning repetitions, drawls of joy
And emphases of frantic freedom, before light ends
And heaps of night are growing.

But if this yearly, only licensed unity,
Linking arms, the love of the other
Leapt from that shore across the rebel sea,
Then marry with their only brotherhood —
All found, all solidness, on the mainland.

Tobago, 1969

CARACAS

On a continent again,
And as the bus roars out
Towards the mountains,
Crashing down the freeway
Through towers and great lights
Reaching the tops of invisible hills
That I know are there behind the darkness —
Space and distance have returned,
And for a moment I forget about
Islands.

                              Venezuela,   1969.

ESSEQUIBO

Docility seems unthinkable here,
With only the coast, lying on the margin
Of the impenetrable,
Killed of its menaces.

Georgetown, in the combed fringe
Of a black, matted growth.
Some white, wooden gestures
Bound for impermanence in the creeping sweat.

So the rivers are your arteries,
Parting your forest, sloping to the sea.
Smothered green deeps, black and brown,
The heraldry of a white man's fear.

Rivers that do not expose
Themselves, but flow like devils
Under their blank surfaces,
Ashamed of their intransigence.

Essequibo,
The name is enough to warn,
As you sink further inside
Its awesomeness of palling beauty,
Or swim in its liquid rust
And scan for lips of fear
Crashing your chest against its fallen greenheart .

Bartica, Guyana. 1969

THE SHOEMAKER'S SON

Peace Corps boy,
You look down on me and smile
And you seem to love me.
But what is the use of your love
From your kind, blue, foreign eyes
If your face is so far above me?
I cannot reach you
With my legs like this,
So you have to bend to me,
And even though your eyes look into mine,
I see their corners staring at my legs,
And they look frightened, Peace Corps boy,
I see them looking down to my ankles
As my legs are sprawled straight, each side of me
At corners from my hips
And my heels point to where my toes should be,
Making nonsense of their nature,
As my limbs weave like tangled branches
Between the leather-ends on the baked mud
Of my father's house.

My father makes shoes —
You have often said how good they are
On your weekly visits.
How the suede feels like cropped fur
On the back of a small animal,
And how it looks as yellow as the ground.
And today you brought a canvas picture of the Pope
To give to the family,
For shining from the rough walls
Inside the room where we eat and sit,
And smiling at me — like you do.
My sisters run around and play with you
And my small brother fetches you a chair
As my mother hurries in her anxious pleasure

And my father beams with pride —
As we entertain you in our parched yard.
But I, the firstborn, can only watch you from my earth,
And think about your kind eyes
As you ask my father if his shoes are selling well,
And my mother, if she likes the picture
And you tell my sisters they are looking pretty
And me, you ask, how am I?
Yo, Teem?
Estoy fregundo con esta maldita vida.

Cucuta, Colombia. 1969.

MUSEUM OF GOLD

Here there are fountains
And concrete walks
And stone gardens
Newly shaped.

There is a new house
With shelves of gold,
And rooms which glow all sides
With its effulgence.

So, here are men with grey suits,
And cars pass
And people pass
Nonplussed by gold.

They have perused
They have studied,
They have been amazed
There was ever so much gold.

Boy in raggy clothes here,
Outside the place of gold here,
On the steps of the lobby of riches here,
With head in his crutch crying
He sits shattered.

                    Bogota, Colombia. 1969

EL DORADO

I found El Dorado this morning,
I got a lift up there in a beer lorry,
And a brewery man led me to the place
As I puffed and wheezed with my lowland lungs
When he set a fast, mountain pace.

I pointed down and gasped 'El Dorado'.
He looked at me and said, 'Senor?'
So I pointed down again with a more perplexed joy,
And he told me through his golden teeth —
Yes, the lake was pretty.

Where a queen had hurled her stark remorse
And men had tossed their gold and emeralds,
Others had thrown their empty beer bottles,
Rolling down the slope, and glinting with the rest,
In unseen piles of men's treasures.

So we walked down to meet the lorry,
And I walked up to the driver
As he smiled with the small gun in his belt,
That was tucked beneath his underpants
As he made out his invoices.

I pointed up, and said 'El Dorado',
And my arm was stabbing the hill and the lake.
He nodded, and with a yellow smile
He pressed a bottle into my hands,
And the label made me gasp and laugh.

I found El Dorado this morning,
Perched and sunken in a lifeless crater,
Shining up to me with a green, stagnant glow,
When I had tumbled up the hill
And reached the rim that should have blazed with gold.

Guatavita, Colombia. 1969.

SAILING HOME

I had found some strong strands of harmony
In my last few months of America,
But here, on the boat home,
I find it difficult to keep those remembrances warm,
When as soon as I boarded I caught a certain sense
Of the armament people wear to protect themselves.
And in the ship's bar,
The blacks on the left
And the whites on the right
In an uncertain truce ignored one another —
Jamaicans, coming home, left their bitternesses with me,
And told me about an England they left,
And colour bars in Kent, their children
Pinched and pushed like pariahs in primary schools.
And a Nigerian with a doctorate in Law
Told me that what we saw the day before in Curacao,
When black men had burnt gaping holes
In the shops of Willemstadt, and carved up the stores
Of rich, white, Dutch merchants in the relief of revenge —
That, he said, was the only way for his brothers.
And with beautiful Trinidad girls
Bouncing to cracked, Spanish music,
And with stumpy, rigid Venezuelans scowling,
And Spanish nuns and priests half benign
But blessing themselves as bare thighs of English girls
Spice their fishy meals,
And a Spaniard offering to fight me
With great Castilian chivalry
Because I had stolen Gibraltar from him,
And young Colombianos drinking themselves
To new, European worlds that I can only see
As gone moments to which I must return —
We move on, over the Atlantic.

And now, aboard this boat,
I am in an airlock between two worlds,
And I cannot remember what came before,
And what comes after is as uncertain
As my journey outwards to find the mainland.
But I know my soul must stamp
To find its air above
The stones of systems' senses
Which do not breathe love.

TN Montserrat, Atlantic Ocean. 1969

Part 2

HOME

BRICK DESH
(For Ron, Linda and Nancy)

Cursing, scrambling shapes of men
Stagger past with bottles sticking
From marsupial pockets.

While kicking boys with balls
Take their zig-zag space
And contest for streets with them.

And here
On fruitstained, methstained corners,
Small men with brown skins
Huddle and gesticulate.

This is their country,
Bounded by dim streets
And shops with shiny coloured fruit
Pressed against the window glass
They have a nation here.

Young men run the roads
Passing angry sheets
Of swirling shapes that speak

Outside the cinema
Inside the cafes
Through the curried air
BANGLA DESH they say,
And men become alive.

Bangla Desh
Found in black brick valleys
Of Spitalfields,
An exile to decay.

It is a long recognition
For the people here
To see themselves in you,
Passing,
Pushing prams, carrying bags
Or reading newspapers
Sunk in their life,
They only look
Or smile, or frown
Do they see their own fight yours?

Their fight
Made hidden by this weight of grey
Pressing submission
Pressing forgetfulness
The smothering of years
The walls of brick
The slow crush of city power
Coming down airlessly.

Tell me brothers
Talking all the bricklight through,
Bring your words and faces to me
Bangla Desh is our land too.

1970

FOR STEPHEN McCARTHY

Running Stephen's head
Smashed against the steel
Of his own city.
Put out your hand from the blue sleeve
A life stops here.

Learning children's heads
Battered by grey men
Against examination posts,
Streamed down dark rivers
Lifeflows separated
Lifepowers delegated.

Beginning to believe
Truth comes in crunches
To the head,
And its concealment
In smiling comfort,
Office chairs.

For those born
Where dying brick
And soaring concrete
And outside men
Cover your life with blows.

Sing for your city
Make its streets love you
It is yours
Only yours.

1971

STEPNEY PLANE TREES

What nurtured you?
Some people say
The air which makes you beautiful
Is killing the world.

Your leaves are girls' faces
Your leaves soften London.
Your mottled trunk, peeling face
Tells of your stoicism.
Your itchy-backs make me laugh
Hanging like ear-rings,
And when they fall
Singing children kick them down the road.

How can you grow in this air?
How can you flourish while
Rushing artics, roaring engines
Give you your breath?

A city's beauty is a brave beauty.

1971

BUS OF SMILES
('To 'Sweet Georgia Brown')

I got on a bus today
It was a bus of smiles,
It chugged off down Commercial Road
I could have gone for miles.

The conductor was a pakky man,
He laughed and smiled and talked,
The rush-hour people squeezed in tight —
Down that street no one walked.

Every face was close together
Brown and white and black,
People near to one another
No one turning back.

At New Road people clambered on,
At Watney Street they queued,
But on the bus they all squeezed in
And made a happy mood.

You might think that things were rough
With so many people on,
Standing dozens up the aisles,
Such a bustling throng —

I think it was a people jam,
But people jammed in joy,
The pakky man had given us
A bus we could enjoy.

As I jumped off at Arbour Square
He winked an eye at me,
I laughed and jumped and saw the sun
Shining on the trees.

I got on a bus today
It was a bus of smiles,
It chugged off down Commercial Road
I could have gone for miles . . .

1971

DISCO

Now, on a dais in the corner of the bar
Sits King Technology,
Controlling all sounds
Ruling all movement
Adjusting all moods.

As new notes pass over the formica
The songs have gone, as if
They are irrelevant, hindrances
To contact.
The sharing now is hair and clothes,
Flash new mannequins
To break the old ways.

They like the king here,
They like his choices,
His knobs and discs and amps
Find approval.

While comes the machine
And goes the tune and voice,
Reaching into his rack for more selections
The king shows more beneficence.

But, ah, down the road
Saturday night and the Queen's Head,
And old docker, suit, collar and tie
Sinatra-like, sings it his way
On a painted platform, as the piano rattles.

The song, like autobiography,
Means something to him.

'The record shows, I took the blows
And did it my way.'

The listeners, their ears in respect, know.
'We know you did mate,
We all tried it our way,
Every one of us'.

A vindication.
Life defended in words and notes
Of a Saturday evening,
Dressed up to justify,
People speak of themselves, and their world
Through vessels made their own.

The sweat runs from the docker's face,
The song was his anthem,
His seconds, minutes, years of struggle
This consciousness broke his love
Not false fortune-making songs
To crack all their dignities.

Only their words, their world, their way.

1972

NO RECRUITING SONG
(to 'Galway Bay')

Please don't go across the sea to Ireland,
Please don't go down Ballymurphy way,
Don't listen to the bullets flying madly
For British soldiers go where bosses say.

The Ulster lads who walk the streets of Belfast
Come from the same world you know every day,
They're working class and struggling out of school-chains,
And looking hard for jobs to get their pay.

Why go and fight them when they live as you do?
Why go and fight your brothers from the Falls?
Why go and fight the boys who are your comrades
Around the bombed-out bricks of Belfast walls.

For Alex, Kevin,Seamus are your schoolmates,
And they've got troops against them night and day,
So give them your support and free their people
And get the soldiers out their country's way.

1972

STREET MUSICIAN

By the unhappy dance of the Spitalfields fire,
Shivering men and rotting fruit
Would warm themselves
One morning I was posting letters —
A name stuck in my back, and up jumped a man.
Out of the flames I lost his face —
Then stubble-smiling, heavy breathing,
'It's nice to be nice', he said.

Where are you Banjo, where are you now?
One day you disappeared,
You weren't sitting on a fruit box in Puma Court
With your bass drum standing beside you,
And Suzie sitting, her tongue panting, her eyes only looking.

That morning you slipped on ice and said,
'In the Winter the weather gets you,
In the Summer the police get you,'
And the Boys, their heads drooping,
Risen grey from their skippers
Nodded agreement as they knelt before ashes
While market porters pulled their working days —
There's no romance in dossing,
Even with a drum, kazoo and dog,
Strumming a banjo down the Lane,
Blacking out the worry on your hundred faces,
Making struggle neutral, nonchalant
With clown's clothes, picked up anywhere.

Surgical spirits, the morning draught of Art,
Or cider shared around the doorsteps,
And the pulsating stops, the man begins —
And Art as stamina, Banjo,
Through war, marriage, unemployment, self, a million songs,

Genius surviving inside seeping cellar walls
Inside gagged mouths of condemned doors
Blindfolded eyes of corrugated windows
Booming through a broken drum and well-worn songs,
Through air thick with the last of men —
Scouse sounds throb where print could never reach
And streets it never thought to reach,
Where Art is hedging, beating Death
At every evening's bedless search for sleep
And feeling through the day.

Be lucky Banjo,
Be lucky tomorrow.

                                        1972

JUNIPER STREET (for Rob)

One night, when the pubs were finished
We wandered through hoardings,
Fields of rubble, padlocked terraces
Of a smashed neighbourhood world.

Tenement trunks gaped with
The wounds of demolition.
Broken windows, starry cutting holes
We looked through,
Down Cable Street, Juniper Street.

Cliffs of dead brick above us,
In a back yard, in a hole of rubble
A spark still glowed from the breakers' fire.
We blew it, fed it, nurtured it
And it blazed.

What were we in that firelight?
Bearded faces, interlopers,
Some new kind of vagrants
Searching for reasons and
Finding changes,
But unalone, together.

We added our stones, hurling
To the broken glass.
Brought more dark, cracking wood
To a nourishing fire,
And shared the flames it gave us.

Now Juniper Street is gone.
New planning, new glass and concrete
Make new places, new neighbours
New identities.

And you are going too
To the back of the world
From where you came.
And in your brown plains,
Aussie cities, wide beaches

When you live and have your children,
Do not discount these things
That once, but always are your world.

                    1972

STRIKE OF WORDS
(Stepney, May 28th, 1971)

Anyone can write a poem, I still hold that,
But you children, sharply organised,
You made your words strike,
The words of your class march
Past middle-class poet-cynics
Shaking their heads, declaring
'Poetry can do nothing,
It makes nothing happen'.

Yes, *their* poetry can do nothing,
Morosely making nothing of the world,
But yours, wed to the march
Can take it over.

Priests who lived for learning shackles
And dullards hanging on to power
Saw their enemies in you, in us,
And with your shouting, loyal words
You blew them over with your poetry.

These children made me what I am,
Their words carved me out a new mind —
I work to make myself
Worth the winning.

Magnificent children,
Sons and daughters of
The future's implacable equity:
I am in love with your clarity
I am in love with your Class.

                                        1972

TO RAMONA, SHARON, MAXINE, KAREN, LESLEY, JANET, CAROLINE, PAULINE, DARSHAN, MARION AND ALL THE OTHERS ...

Don't let them use you because you are pretty,
Don't let them sew you up in offices,
Trap you in the letters of a typewriter,
Tempt you by an underground advertisement
Towards glamorous bosses.
Show them you are minds, you are women,
You are power, you are people,
Not buttons to be pressed, legs to be fancied,
Fashions to be changed, objects to be used.
Fight for your class, not for your enemy,
Fight for yourselves, not for your employer,
Fight for your lives, not for your haters,
And you will find your lovers waiting,
Waiting on this mainland.

1972

BRIXTON ISLAND
(For Mel and Graham)

This is a new island,
I see the same faces of underdevelopment here.
But black and white —
There is a consummation in this island,
Scattered colours of the oppressed become one class
Between the legs of railway arches,
And energy pulsates and stiffens with an exile's soul
From Desmond's Hip City, reaching over market stalls
And yams of estrangement.

But here it is. From wandering, struggling, escaping,
This is what we come to
And this is what we make, our island
Like the others we have left behind,
Black islands, white islands, islands of the mind —
We are all here, and this is ours,
Our lives shall sing of this.

The mainland of our class
Connects us with the world —
We are also of the world,
Struggling island of the dispossessed.
Our world, the third world of men
Who return for reclamations,
Making their islands mount to the height of their wills
Like Toussaint's army in a foreign land.

This will be Brixton Island,
Island of the mainland.

1973

ASSEMBLY

Hearing these voices sing to an unknown god
In the false rhythms of rote and habit,
Seeing these children's faces, this spectrum of the world
Worshipping only whiteness, classness, bossness;
Faraway faces mouthing the anthems of an enemy —
I have looked towards the other cheek,
And have heard other words, other sounds
That have changed my curses into joy . . .

I heard the Internationale this morning in assembly,
I saw the world's working class singing together,
I heard their daily solidarity sweeping over South London.
I saw African forests in Flora's eyes, Nigerian rivers
    gleaming through their huge hearts,
India's masses in the dark, growing strands of Mahnoor's hair,
Trench Town, Dungle agonies making to resist and struggle
In a host of Jamaican skins moving to each other.
I saw Belfast brick in white Irish faces mortared by rebellion,
South-East Asian ways of fire in a Hong Kong eye,
Mountain fighters in Cypriot smiles,
And London voices, voices pounding from grey streets
Tenanted by men who built and made this city,
All singing, the words of belongingness
Surging from the lips of children . . .

Now, teachers under the world school's roof,
Don't mystify them, give them truth,
Don't give them morning hymns or words
Of Lord of Lords or holy swords
Or God in whiteness or in glory —
Don't mystify them with that story.
Give them the skills to know their brain
And power enough for them to gain
Their world for them and all their brothers —
Teach them facts, not lies that smother

Up their streets and words and skins
And hide the realness of those things.
Give them strength to push their class
Over the rich man, over the boss,
Over the heaps of lies called Knowledge —
Give them truth, and give them courage.

1973

STEPNEY STRENGTH

Tomorrow I saw
People in crowds bravely together,
Flowing down the two arteries of Stepney —
Whitechapel Road, Commercial Road,
Moving towards a huge convergence
Somewhere over the scars of Aldgate.

Tomorrow I wondered
How these people joined together, lifting oppression away,
How they lost their isolation, their aloneness,
How they linked arms and breaths and voices
Making the noise of new people
As they called out to passing shoppers in the Waste.
The energy of their voices blew and sucked at the sails of the
                                        market stalls,
Making the fruit swell with proud juice
And the dusty flowers lose their dullness —
As women flung away their shopping bags
                    and their plastic bags
                    and their carrier bags
All spilling on the flagstones, swept away by the wind
                                of ten thousand legs.

Tomorrow I celebrated
The joy of children making the streets their own,
Leaping up from debris, alleys and schools,
Clasping the hands of their teachers
Splintering the divisions between them
Laughing down the walls which separate them
As they came together in tributary streams up the side
                                streets of Stepney,
Making endless confluences with the people river.

Tomorrow I marvelled
As the crowd passed Nelson Street,

To see unmarried mothers kissing Social Security clerks —
Hugging between them
The dissolution of their fears and claims
And pushing prams together
Down Settles Street where downcast men walking in circles
                              and waiting for work
Lost their giddiness, lost their search for bosses
Finding employment in each other
Moving, thronging with the rest.

Tomorrow I remembered
Rag trade girls pouring from the factories
The skirts they made themselves streaming from their own hips
The blouses blowing from their own breasts,
Giving leather coats, freshly stitched, to their comrades,
And East End beauty glowed beneath the greyness of
                              condemned shops —
As Punjabi men peered from Hessel Street,
Running from the sweet and curry shops
Milling in the doorways of Halal butchers
Piling from the Palaseum cinema
Quickly conferring on the pavements
Grasping the arms of Bengali brothers
Calling their wives from their paraffin-heated room-cells —
And made their brown skins shine with the London sun
Mixing with the white, shifting faces of the river
And jumping in the mainstream.

Tomorrow my eyes looked above.
The windows of London Hospital were flung open
And ill people, old people, ending people
Flew their hopes onto the heads of the crowds
Threw out their hearts to catching children
Blew their kisses into the singing air
As their nurses waved their love.

Tomorrow I sang
Of sleeping dossers in Itchy Park
Waking with new mind-muscles

Smashing out of the bottles which imprisoned them
Scattering their broken past like the glass around them
Watering the sickly grass with unwanted meths
Moving without thought of begging,
Sweeping defeat from their tired eyes
And raising them like banners from drooping faces —
To see their neighbours in great shoals passing them.

Tomorrow I rejoiced
As dockers heaved up from Leman Street, Mansell Street
From riversides they had reclaimed themselves,
Thrusting aside the lies of speculators,
Taking possession of their struggling history
And working again, willed by new comradeship
In the strength of a collective arm.

Tomorrow I wrote poems
To the Chicksand tenants, the Bigland tenants
Running from their buildings, singing on their balconies,
Hurling their words from the tops of the Watney Street towers,
Spreading in great ranks down Cannon Street Road and
                                  Brick Lane
Saying to each other, 'It is the time. NOW is the time',
And arming themselves with each other.

Tomorrow I saw
The meeting of two great rivers,
I saw people like deep flowing waters
Joining and becoming one —
I saw how mighty we are
I saw how we will win
I saw LOVE STRENGTH
        ONE STRENGTH
        CLASS STRENGTH
        STEPNEY STRENGTH
        OUR STRENGTH

1973

WELL MET

I found a comrade right round here
Amongst the people, streets and beer,
Flowing down to Shadwell Park
And round and round me in the dark.

She had a clear and speaking touch,
I didn't need to *think* of much,
She only told me who I was
And laughed when I said I was lost.

She said, 'think what you've found with me,
I'll grow inside you like a tree,
My leaves will fall on all your friends
And men who hate you won't pretend.

They'll only fight with bourgeois code
And words which take a no through road,
But you've got me, and you are strong —
You'll find I'll love you all life long'.

I said, 'I trust your words and frame
But now I have to know your name
To help me struggle, now hope has risen . . .'
She said, 'My name is Socialism'.

1973

THE FOURTH QUARTER

From the cocoon breaks the monster,
The world lets him breathe again.
His poison falls back in the memory,
He breaks the day, the noon darkens.

Now is the fourth quarter:
The century ends that promised us equity.
The winds sweep through the branches,
The leaves rustle with warnings.
The crosses clank on the national flag,
Their clangs make the sound of marching iron.

To the beat of chauvinism and voracious nostalgia
The fascists reassemble.
Their white slogans wave in our streets,
Their scientists move to prove their prejudices
With synthetic fact, designed for genocide.

The beasts are rampant in Chile:
Their allies move in their British cadres,
Planning their hatred in army words —
Now is the calling,
The time of dithering is done,
The here, the now, the us!

We, who have lived the guise, beguiled by security,
Fooled by the affluence of the skin,
Know the facade drops away, reality tightens.
We, who have waited for this calling,
We the readers, the rockers
We the teds, the demonstrators,
We the banners, the mods,
We the marchers, the skinheads,

We the hippies, the hooligans,
We, the waiting generations,
The diverted ones, the untried ones,
The pawns of mode, the children of welfare:
Throw away your shades, move with your brothers —
The time of dithering is done!